An Otter's G

To Being Obnoxiously Happy

Hiram J. Bertoch

An Otter's Guidebook

An Otter's Guidebook

To Being Obnoxiously Happy

Editor: Judy Banks ‖ Editor: Karrie Robison
Cover art by B. H. ‖ Cover Design By F. Wiggen
Expert Reader: Pam Berry
Photography: Leah-Anne Thompson ‖ Photography: Strokket

All rights reserved. No part of this publication may be reproduced, stored in a retrieval system, or transmitted in any form or by any means, electronic, mechanical, photocopying, recording, or otherwise, without written permission of the author. Except by a reviewer who may quote brief passages or reproduce illustrations in a review with appropriate credits.

www.OtterGuidebook.com

Library of Congress Control Number: 2016955225
Copyright © 2016 Piedmont Pages Imprint
10 9 8 7 6 5 4 3 2
ISBN: 978-0-9845736-4-6
ISBN: 0-9845736-4-X

Imprint: Piedmont Pages
Hunter, Utah

To my three sons

It is my deepest hope that you will each follow the counsel in this book and that as a result you will experience absolute and total joy throughout your lives.

To my four daughters

It is my deepest hope that you will each marry men who follow the counsel in this book, and that as a result you and your children will be treated the way that you deserve to be treated.

An Otter's Guidebook

Author's Note

As you read An Otter's Guidebook To Being Obnoxiously Happy, you will find that throughout this book I have shared a number of personal stories and experiences.

I am neither famous nor important enough to have anyone care about the finer details of my life, and therefor feel somewhat uncomfortable in making so much of this book about myself.

However, these experience form the basis of my understanding of this topic. In order to fairly and adequately discus happiness and what leads a man towards being happy I couldn't separate my experiences from my understanding.

I therefor ask for the readers indulgence and forgiveness for my having so frequently shared personal details about my own life.

An Otter's Guidebook

Introduction

Have you ever stopped and watched a group of playful sea otters interact?   Next time you are at a zoo, an aquarium, or near the coast it would be well worth your time to pause for a moment and thoughtfully consider their actions. There is a lot to be learned about happiness from a [1]bevy of sea otters.

They are playful and energetic. They have boundless energy, and a natural love of life.

No matter what is going on in the world around them or what setbacks or obstacles they may face, sea otters are

---

1   A group of otters is often referred to as a bevy, just a s a group of cows is referred to as a herd.

determined to be happy, and to enjoy every moment of their lives as fully as absolutely possible.

It is enough to make a grown man sick!

Really? Do you have to be THAT happy! Is it necessary to be so despicably giddy every single moment of your life?

Annoying little rodents!

In addition to being obnoxiously happy, otters have another admirable trait that is worth pondering. Otters are uncommonly affectionate towards one another. Even among animals that live in packs, prides, herds, or flocks, a bevy of otters stands out as a uniquely warm and loving place, where there are plenty of snuggles to go around.

They love to cuddle! Just watch them! It won't take very long before one of the otters that you are observing will seek out another in order to give or receive love.

They rub their little fur covered snouts against the cheeks of their family members, or lie side by side as they rest their little heads on each other, forming tangled knots of little furry arms, noses, and tails.

2

Sea otters don't get embarrassed by love. They don't worry what the rest of their furry little companions might think of their tenderness. A family of otters knows how important love is, and so they seek it out, and willingly give it to each other unconditionally.

In this book you will find ten lessons, taken from the lives of otters, that will guide a man towards obnoxiously unapologetic happiness.

While this book is written with men in mind, many of these lessons also apply to women. Otters provide a great example upon which we can all model our own lives.

Do you want to be happy?

Do you want to be obnoxiously and infectiously upbeat? Do you want to be so relentlessly giddy that you annoy your family and friends? To the point that they want to puke after mere moments of exposure to your boundless enthusiasm for life?

Happiness is an emotion that naturally and inevitably increases, when you build your life on a foundation of certain universal principles.   It is not an emotion kept in reserve and only available to little furry otters.

Just as assuredly as we can predict that our lawns will grow taller if we water them, so too can we predict that if you build your life on these principles, that you will unavoidably end up sickeningly happy.

You will still experience sorrow, loss, and disappointment. But as a whole your life will be wonderful, and the positives will vastly outweigh any hardships that you may experience.

Even otters sometimes have bad days, or even a bad season. But wounds heal, time marches on, and when taken as a whole, their lives are rather jovial.

Likewise, by building your life on the same foundation that they do, the difficult times will be softened, and will be far outnumbered by the good things in your life.

You will unavoidably find that you are happy!

Chapter 1

Never Swim Alone

Personal Story

My heart beat heavy and slow. I was too worried to take notice of the shadows cast across the dark road. Distorted silhouettes of trees and houses, drawn in the moonlight.

As I walked towards no particular destination, it felt as though a thousand circus elephants were using my body as a trampoline. Jumping up and down, while I gasped for relief.

I knew better than to stay up so late, and there was little doubt in my mind that I would have to pay for my early morning stroll the next day. But knowing that I should be in bed, and actually being able to go to sleep were two very different things.

Exhaustion didn't begin to describe how my body felt. Nor did that word take into account the emotions that were tormenting my mind, and rolling around inside my head.

I desperately needed to rest I needed to escape both the physical exhaustion and the mental despair. Yet these were the two very things working against me, and keeping me awake.

The burden and gravity of my recent mistakes were weighing heavily on my mind. I had spent hours lying silently in bed reviewing the events that led to my error in judgment, hoping to find a way that I could fix the problems that my decisions had created.

I laid their in agony and desperation, tossing from side to side, until I eventually gave up, opened my eyes, rubbed my hand through my hair, and decided to see if a walk would help me clear my mind.

I suppose that what I hoped was that as I walked I might find some dark secret place where I could tuck away my problems so that I would then be able to return home with a clear slate, free from their heavy grasp.

As I walked, I thought about the business that I had built up over the previous 16 years. It had grown far more successful than I had ever dreamed or intended. I hadn't set out to be a successful business man. I was just having fun, doing something that I enjoyed.

We were now an interntional company, and the worldwide leader in our market. Up until a few days earlier, I had felt that nothing could possibly threaten that. A confidence that had led me to take what I thought had been a safe and calculated risk.

I had directed tens of thousands of company dollars to be spent in pursuit of a business deal that if we could make work, would lead to a profit of potentially several million dollars. The odds seemed high that we would be successful in our efforts.

Now that the deal had fallen through however, and the money that we had invested in it had evaporated almost overnight I was left feeling distraught over the financial setback.

It wasn't enough to put us out of business, but it would really hurt. Things would get tighter for awhile. Other opportunities would have to be passed up on, because we wouldn't have the funds or means to take advantage of them. This would delay our future growth and affect the lives of my employees in a potentially very negative way.

As my heavy footsteps carried me aimlessly through the neighborhoods that surrounded my home, I replayed the events in my mind over and over again. Where had I gone wrong? What should I have done differently? How had I allowed myself to spend so much money on what would in the end yield absolutely nothing in return?

My mind twisted tighter, like a washcloth getting wrung out, and as it did so, the despair in my heart began to grow into a sort of panic.

Finally, feeling utterly defeated, and further than ever from finding any comfort or relief, I turned around and began to slowly make my way back home.

After several minutes I once again found myself in my bedroom. Still feeling forlorn I quietly slid myself back into bed, careful so as to not disturb my wife.

As I laid by her side, something totally unexpected and truly memorable to me happened. My wife Anna rolled over, and put her arm around me.

It was magical! Her embrace did what hours of fruitless contemplation had failed to do. Instantaneously all the panic, stress, and worry all melted away. Like a bee drawn towards a beautiful flower, I snuggled in closer to her, and marveled at the power of her embrace.

it was just money. The company would survive. We were still on top of our niche market. I wouldn't have to lay anyone off. My mortgage would get paid. My kids would eat. Why had I worried so much! It wasn't really that big of a deal!

Anna was sound asleep. She had no idea of the effect that she had on me. But her gentle touch made all the difference that night. As she held me, my worries evaporated into thin air and disappeared completely. I felt at peace. Life was not just going to be okay, it was going to be truly wonderful!

Otter Lesson # 1
It's Dangerous To Swim Alone

There are a lot of predators in the ocean, and it just so happens that a sea otter makes a perfect bite-sized snack!

In a world where danger can come from both around you, and also from the depths below, the more eyes that you have keeping watch, the better!

It is dangerous and foolish to spend too much time in the ocean alone.

Otters are one of the few animal species that form monogamous partnerships that last throughout their lifetimes. Beginning when they are about two years old, otters look for a partner with whom they will share the rest of their lives. Tenderly supporting and caring for each other and for their offspring.

They work together to find food, fend off danger, and draw comfort and enjoyment from their companionship.

You and I were likewise not meant to wander through our lives alone. We have a fundamental need to share our lives with a companion. A best friend, who has our best interest at heart, who looks out for us, and who we can be tender with. A precious soul with whom we are comfortable sharing every aspect of our lives with.

Sometimes as men, we wrongly believe that being tough means closing others out from our emotions. We get the foolish idea in our heads that showing emotion equates to showing weakness.

To be clear, there is nothing wrong with quiet confidence. Self-confidence is important. If these are the definitions that we use for the word "tough" then we are on solid ground as men. However, if we define being tough as feeling no sadness, or as only feeling anger, then we are never going to realize true joy.

When we are alone with our wives, our guard should go down. If we are truly going to benefit from our relationship with her, then she has to be the one person that is allowed inside of our personal walls of protection that we as men build.

I am not suggesting that you have to cry in front of your wife.

What I am suggesting is only that you communicate how you feel to her. If you are stressed out, then she should know it. If you are worried about money then you should have mentioned this to her. If you are going through a difficult trial at work, she should know why.

It is as simple as talking to her, and sharing with her those things that you would never share with anyone else.

How can she be your best friend, if you don't entrust her with your deepest secrets? More importantly, how can she fulfill her role as your greatest source of comfort, peace, and support, if you don't confide in her?

Do you see that it is you who suffers the most, when you choose to conceal your feelings from your wife!

To the rest of the world you can be a solid slate of granite. An emotionless monolith that always knows exactly what to do, and confidently walks through life never questioning which steps that they are supposed to take. That is fine. The rest of the world does not need to be let inside your walls. But she does!

Notice that the word "she" is singular. Being your best friend, your soul mate, and your closest confidant is not a role that multiple women can play! Nor can this role be filled for a short period of time, and then easily replaced by another partner.

The longer that you are with someone, the deeper that your love for them will grow, and the more that you will feel that you can trust them. On your wedding day, you will believe that you are in love. Twenty years later you will have opened up new dimensions on your love that you couldn't even have imagined existed before. Though I haven't yet made it there, I suspect that couples who have been married for 65 years have a depth of love and mutual kinship that is all the more unfathomable.

Yes, you can start over with a new partner. But doing so, starts this clock over again. If you are presently alone, then get started building your life with someone as soon as you can.

If you already have a companion then do everything in you power to hold on to her! Don't throw away the years of memories and experiences that the two of you have created together. What you have with her is so much deeper than what you would find with a newer partner.

It is true that the excitement of a new relationship can be fun, and seem appealing, but that newness will wear off very quickly. Following after that newness will lead you towards a succession of empty relationships that never allow you to reach your full potential as a man.

Stay with the woman who is currently at your side. As you do so, the excitement of a new relationship will be dramatically overshadowed and surpassed by a depth of love, compassion, and joy that can only be understood by those men who were smart enough to stick it out during hard times, and who remained faithful to their wives even when a seemingly more exciting opportunity walked by.

If you want to be happy then find a woman who you can love. Marry her, and then make her the focus of the rest of your life.

Don't be like the many fools that unfortunately abound in today's world, who do not see the value in marriage. Men who move from one meaningless relationship to another leaving a trail of broken promises in their wake.

Then there are those men who may stay with a single partner, but who never fully commit themselves to her through the act of marriage. These men might believe that their relationship stands on equal footing with other men who are married to their partners.

They have after all remained together as boyfriend and girlfriend for years. However, their relationship lacks permanency. Without marriage, they are still nothing more than roommates. Either one could walk out of the relationship tomorrow without any recourse or legal consequence.

Marriage means that you and your wife now belong to each other. You are now much more than just roommates.

Beginning on your wedding day, you no longer function as two separate people. You share the same last name, the same house, the same bank account, the same bed, the same children, and if you are wise, each others deepest secrets and confidences.

Marriage means that you are committed to each other on a scale that far exceeds that of just a boyfriend and a girlfriend. You are so committed to one another, that you were willing to legally join your souls together.

If you truly love her, then ask yourself what it is that is keeping you from committing to marriage? Why are you withholding that part of yourself? Why aren't you giving your whole self to her?

So far we have talked about men who move from one relationship to another, as well as those men who do carry on a single long term relationship, but without the benefit of a binding marriage certificate.

There is one more category of men, who deprive themselves of a fullness of their own potential for happiness. These are the men who choose to put off forming any kind of intimate relationships whatsoever. These men choose to remain single, until such time as they accomplish some future goal. These goals can take on many different forms.

For example, I have heard of men choosing to avoid any romantic relationships until after they are financially established, or until after they have finished college, or have purchased a home.

This decision to put off marriage until some arbitrary goal has been accomplished is one of the most foolish choices that these men will ever make.

Firstly, it deprives these men of the comfort that a sweet dear wife would have provided them during those years when they needed that comfort the most.

Young adulthood is a time when your paycheck will likely be smaller than at any other point in your life. As a result, this is a time when financial burdens will be at their highest levels.

Some men think that they act wisely by putting off marriage until they can "afford" it. The reality is that they are only making their journey that much more difficult. With a partner at their side, the financial stresses of early adulthood would have been so much easier to deal with, and to get through.

A second thing to consider are the huge variety of choices that you will be making during your time as a young adult. Choices that will have a profound impact on your lifelong routines and lifestyle.

Little things like what your daily schedule looks like, how you like to spend your free time, where you like to go on vacation, how and when you do your laundry, and ten thousand other tiny details of life that quickly add up.

By putting off marriage until after all of these small and large choices have been made and all your routines have been established, you forgo the guidance and input of your future best friend and lifelong companion.

You could have solved life's problems together. Grown interested in the same hobbies, discovered mutual routines that worked well for both of you. It would have been easier and felt almost natural.

By waiting until after you are established to get married, it means that while you were busy figuring out how to live as an adult, so was she. And as a result, while you fell into your routines, she fell into hers. Two sets of routines and strategies for accomplishing life's tasks that are completely different from one another.

How much more challenging is it going to be to bring your lives together after you have spent a decade or more getting comfortably set in your distinct ways.

How much better off would you have been to have gotten married young, to have enjoyed her next to you on those stressful nights, and to have solved life's challenges

18

together. Learning to function in the adult world together in mutually satisfying routines, that she is as committed to as you are.

Lastly, when you look at your dear wife years later, you will be robbed of the tender knowledge that she stuck with you throughout all those hard times. When your paycheck was not large enough to cover your bills. She was there at your side, supporting you. How much more will you trust and love her as a result?

How much sweeter will your relationship be with her, because you found her early rather than later?

Though the wisdom of the world might suggest otherwise, my advice to you is that you get married young. You owe it to yourself to find your dear sweetheart before life's challenges overwhelm you.

After you find her, love her with all of your heart. Invest every ounce of your soul into your relationship with your wife. Make her the central focus of your life, Share your feelings and thoughts with her. Make her your most trusted friend, and then never ever look back.

Chapter 2
When You Find Her, Commit To Her

Personal Story

It had been years since I had been to San Diego. I had traveled there with my parents as a child, and my wife Anna and I had also brought our own children there on vacation a few times. However, this was the first time that I would be wandering through the city alone.

Due to flight conflicts, I arrived a day earlier than my business required. Which meant that I had a bit of down time to kill. With so many potentially enjoyable activities to choose from in such a beautiful place as San Diego, it was difficult to decide what I wanted to do. After some debate however, I eventually settled upon spending the afternoon kayaking in the ocean.

I was looking forward to leisurely paddling though shark infested waters, exploring sea caves, and skimming across kelp forests. Which is probably why I arrived about 45 minutes early to my appointment at the seaside shop where I was scheduled to rent my gear, and meet my tour guide.

After realizing my error, I had a choice to make. I could either sit and wait in the small wet lobby next to cold dripping wet guests who had just returned, or I could go outside and enjoy the soft and salty ocean breezes and take in the warm sunshine. I choose the latter.

After standing outside by the shop entrance for a few minutes, I got bored, and eventually ended up strolling along a nearby boardwalk. Where I could watch other tourists, browse through a few gift shops, and enjoy the

22

sounds of crashing waves as their powerful thunder-like vibrations mixed with the eager cries of eager and hungry seagulls.

It was a wonderful moment. So much so, that I nearly lost track of time. With 15 minutes left I realized that, I had better hurry back towards my appointment with the kayak outfitter. I quickly retraced my steps back, enjoying, as I walked, the sunlight, and the general feeling of peaceful serenity that one feels in such an inspiring location.

With five minutes left until I needed to check in, I found myself on a particular stretch of sidewalk where I was all alone. No one was in front of, or behind me. I couldn't see anyone. Nor to the best of my knowledge could anyone see me.

My brief solitude was however interrupted after just a few moments. Up a head of me, two very scantily dressed women in what I will refer to as "beach attire" rounded a corner and began walking in the same direction as myself. They were no more than ten feet in front of me.

These two attractive girls didn't notice my presence behind them.

So far as I knew no one I knew could see me. My wife wasn't there. My children were not there. I could have chose to slowly walk behind them, and admire the view. What would it hurt?

I am after all only human! As a result of which I am naturally attracted to members of the opposite gender. What harm could come from admiring these women from a safe distance? My wife would never have to know!

It would be a perfectly natural thing for me as man to avail himself of such fortunate timing and take it in for all that it was worth! Right? Isn't that the natural thing to do? There couldn't be any shame in giving in to my biology could there?

I will not claim that it was an easy thing to do. Because in all honesty it wasn't. It was extremely difficult. It took all of my personal will power, in order to steer myself correctly in that moment.

However, I am proud to say that I didn't look. I honestly didn't. I maintained my focus off to the side, and speed up my pace so that I would pass these women, and then with them behind me, no longer face the temptation of starring.

I remained true to my wife, to my children, and to my own personal goals as a man. I controlled myself, and put my own long term happiness above a few moments of personal gratification that would then have lived forever in my memory, as a moment of weakness, regret, shame, and disappointment.

Otter Lesson # 2
Otters Are Fiercely Monogamous

Male sea otters stay very close to their companions. Perhaps even a little too close! In an effort to keep their slippery females from sliding away into the waves of a constantly turbulent sea, these male otters sometimes bite their companions' snouts and then hold onto them for dear life with their teeth.

For the record, I do not recommend biting your wife's nose, and then pulling her around wherever you go! She most likely will not appreciate that!

Indeed, unless you want your wife to physically harm you, I would probably instead look at this aspect of otter love as a metaphor!

Rather than being physically attached snout to snout, we aught to be mentally and spiritually attached so firmly to our dear wives, that when the waves and trials of life wash over us, they are absolutely unable to separate us from each other.

Is there harm in looking at another woman after you have already found your best friend and committed yourself to her?

Will thinking about other women, flirting with other women, or fantasizing about other women lead to any negative consequences in your life, or in hers?

The answer to these questions is unequivocally yes. Giving in to your natural attraction towards another woman to even the smallest degree is devastatingly harmful to your relationship with your sweetheart, and ultimately undermines both your happiness and her confidence in you.

First and foremost, by giving into your base instincts you betray your best friend's trust. She loves you, and depends absolutely on your being faithful to her.

There is no doubt whatsoever in her mind that you are a knight in shinning armor. She believes herself to be the luckiest woman in the entire world.   She further believes that she is the central focus of your entire life.

Our wives very often believe in us, and trust us far more than we by ourselves merit or deserve.

Are you really going to betray that level of sacred and absolute trust? If she ever found out, how would she feel? How will you feel knowing that your actions crushed her unwavering faith and disappointed her?

You may be thinking to yourself that this counsel only applies if your wife actually finds out about your actions!

You may likewise be thinking that as long as you are careful, and only peaking at women when she is not around, or only fantasizing in the privacy of your own mind, or looking at something as devastatingly harmful as pornography, but only when she is not there to see it, then what she doesn't know won't ever hurt her!

Don't kid yourself. Eventually your wife is going to find out.

If you occasionally sneak looks at other women when you think that no one is watching you, then this habit will grow into something that you will have a difficult time controlling. At some point this habit is inevitably going to betray you.

Someday you will forget that others are around, and out of habit, you will risk sneaking a glance at an attractive woman when your wife or children are present.

You will begin to lose control! Those who you love, and who depend upon you, will see you actions and will question your commitment to your wife and family.

Even in those moments when you truly are alone. Your actions have lasting consequences.

In addition to looking at other women, so to do the secret fantasies of your heart harm your relationship with your wife.

These two personal indulgences cause you to raise your expectations regarding physical attraction to unrealistic levels.

You will then begin to judge your wife against these unrealistic standards. Which will lead to you growing increasingly unsatisfied with a woman who prior to your indiscretions you found to be very beautiful.

We define beauty to ourselves based on those things that we most often look at and think about. Above all, we define beauty based upon those things that we spend the most time cherishing in the secret parts of our minds.

Which leads us to one of the most unfortunate tragedies that will then become your realty.

Had you kept your eyes, thoughts, and fantasies where they belonged, you would have grown to define beauty based on the woman at your side.

Indeed your very definition of what truly is attractive, would be based on the women that you get to be with! You would have grown absolutely convinced that if you were to look up the word "hot" in the dictionary that you would find a picture of you wife!

By including stolen glances of other women in your repertoire of what constitutes your definition of beauty, in the end, you rob yourself of that experience.

Consider for a moment what I am saying. You could have had what you personally and genuinely perceive to be the single and absolute most beautiful woman on the entire planet at your side. A woman who in your sincere opinion was a 10,000 out of 10. More attractive than any super model! But because of your foolish and errant glances elsewhere you ruined that opportunity for yourself.

Your unfortunate choices robbed you of spending your life with the most beautiful woman in the entire world!

As a man, that is a heavy price to pay! All for ten seconds of gratification here and there.

This is however not the only price that you will pay, nor the heaviest. In addition to robbing yourself of spending your life with the single most attractive woman on the face of the planet, you also face another far more serious consequence. You lose the respect of your children.

To them, their mother stands on a pedestal high above all other beings, real or imaginary. They don't care what their mom looks like, how she dresses, or how her personality manifests itself. To a child, their mommy is the

30

single most snugly and wonderful creature in the entire Universe.

Even after they enter adulthood, your children will not comprehend, even in the smallest degree, how you could ever be so foolish as to look at, or have eyes for anyone but their mother. They will see you look at a woman, and as they get older begin to discount you as someone worthy of admiration.

The biggest loss though comes in the form of a diminished relationship with your wife, and a weakened friendship.

How can you share every part of your soul with her, if you are thinking about other women? A truly happy man shares every thought, every concern, every dream with his dear sweet wife.

Are you going to confess to her that you looked at, or flirted with, or thought about another girl in an inappropriate way? If not, how can you say that you are sharing everything that you are with her?

If you can't share every part of your soul with your wife, then there will always be space between you and her. You will then be unable to live as one, but will instead

31

become two separate souls, drifting spiritually apart, and as a result will never feel as close to her as you otherwise could have.

Now, to be fair, no one is perfect. There will be moments in each of our lives when our eyes are going to find their way somewhere that they should not have. Moments when we do not intend, or do not realize that we are betraying our goals, or our personal commitments to ourselves and to our wives.

We are after all men. Our attraction to the opposite gender is real, strong, and very natural. And let's be honest; there are plenty of opportunities in life to see things that we know we shouldn't. At some point you are going to briefly mess up, and glance at things that you will later regret.

In the interest of sharing everything with your companion, should you confess these mistakes to your wife? Should you tell her how attractive the girl was that you were momentarily glancing at?

May I suggest that the answer is yes.

Remember, our goal is to have a level of trust and comfort between us that is so strong that we can and do share everything between us!

However, in order to preserve the strength of your relationship with your wife, and keep yourself focused on the right goals, I suggest that you do this sharing in a smart, straightforward, and honest way.

A way that reinforces her trust in you, and that trains and reinforces your mind's efforts to focus all of your attractions, thoughts, passions and desires on her.

Firstly, as soon as you catch yourself looking somewhere that you shouldn't be looking, regain control, and look away immediately.

Then say to your wife, some variation of "I really hate it when I see women dressed that way. It makes it hard for a guy to keep focused on the things that matter in life. I am so glad that I have you sweetheart!! She is nothing even close to as pretty as you are!" [2]

---

2 Please note that such a comment, made privately between yourself and your wife does not imply that you are blaming the other woman for how she is dressed. Rather, you are simply taking ownership of your own feelings, and acknowledging the reality of where these feelings came from, in a privately spoken comment that remains between you and your wife.

You have acknowledged to your wife that you inadvertently looked at something you regret. That it created an internal struggle for you and that this made you uncomfortable.

You have been honest with her that you didn't appreciate having to deal with that struggle. And that in the end, it was any easy choice for you to choose to put your dear wife ahead of any personal momentary gratification, and that you focused instead on your commitment to her.

Following this pattern reinforces to her that you are worth trusting. while reminding you of how you aught to act, think, and feel in these unavoidable situations.

After awhile you won't have to say the words out loud. After hearing you go though this process ten or twenty times your wife will recognize the expressions on your face, she will know without any doubt what you are thinking.

She will watch you shake your head silently, and will smile inwardly as she thinks about how lucky she is to be married to a man who is 100% committed to only her.

It is worth emphasizing again, that you are the one who benefits from dedicating yourself to a single lifelong partner.

Consider it from a very selfish perspective. If you choose to take another path, and to some degree or another withhold commitment to your wife, then it is you who will ultimately pay the heaviest price.

You could have been married to the woman who you personally find to be the most attractive woman on Earth. You could have maintained the respect of your children. You could have had a personal closeness with a best friend that would have bought you unspeakable joy.

The only way that you can avoid losing these blessings is by total and absolute commitment to one single woman throughout your entire lifetime.

As I stated in the previous chapter, it is possible to start over, and build something wonderful with someone new. So long as your intent and focus is on making what you build into something that will last for a lifetime.

If you messed up in the past. Then yes, you have paid a price for those mistakes. That price may be heavy, but it doesn't have to last forever.

Learn from your mistakes, and start over again. This time do it right! This time, make your relationship one that will last forever!

Then in time, you too will find great joy, and happiness.

Chapter 3
Focus On Her Strengths
Her Weaknesses Will Take Care of Themselves

Personal Story

It had been a long trip and I was very tired. I began my journey towards home, departing from Sao Paulo, Brazil almost 20 hours earlier.

My trip home included a bus ride, a taxi ride, a dreadfully uncomfortable plane ride, a six hour layover in a foreign airport, and finally after I was exhausted and irritable, one last long flight towards home.

At last, I thought to myself, I have made it! I was in our hometown airport! All that remained, was to sit on the curb and await the arrival of my wife who was coming to pick me up.

It was only 3:00 pm, but to me, it felt like the middle of the night. As I sat on a hard metal bench in the airport's pickup waiting area, I thought longingly of my soft bed, just a few miles away. Which would be far more comfortable than the last place I had tried to sleep!

Sleeping on a long international flight, had felt more like being a prisoner than like getting rest. Stuffed between strangers, with their seat backs too close to my knees, on a chair with very little padding, was not my idea of a good time.

Just thinking about it made me want to break out into hives and gag. Where was my wife! The very little energy that I had was earnestly dedicated to the hopeful thought that I would soon sink into my own bed, and rest my head on my own familiar pillows.

If she didn't arrive soon, I might collapse right where I was. On to the hot, gum covered concrete sidewalk outside the airport. In that moment, curling up under the bench didn't really sound that bad!

As long as I could stretch out my arms and legs, breath fresh air, and not bump into people that I didn't know, then I could probably have laid just about anywhere, and slept like a baby for hours.

To me, it felt like my wife Anna was taking forever to arrive. However, these feelings were not based in reality. I was just in an impatient mood. The truth was that she had been waiting for me in a nearby parking lot, and after only a few short moments pulled up alongside the curb.

"Hi, how are you?" I sighed, as I slumped into the passenger seat.

"I am glad you are home," she replied in an abrupt though polite manner. In her voice there was a tone of both exhaustion and frustration.

Being a man, and therefor being absolutely convinced that it is always my personal responsibility to solve my wife's problems, by getting to the bottom of whenever she might sound a little irritable, I asked a very stupid question.

"Why are you so ornery?"

Now, in fairness to myself, in my mind I was being supportive. I was also completely exhausted, and thus a little short on common sense.

By the way, in case you are wondering please allow me to clarify that it is ALWAYS a bad idea to ask your wife why she is ornery! Even when you mean well!!

My dear wife Anna, did not get upset with me. She is a softhearted and gentle soul, who is not easily provoked.

Though I would have deserved any remark that she might have made. She simply began to graciously explain that it had been a difficult week for her.

Though my intent in asking such a foolish question was to be supportive, I perceived in her facial expressions and in her tightening voice that the question had not been a helpful one. Nor did it feel supportive to her.

By indirectly being critical of her, I ended up adding to her stress, rather than helping to minimize or reduce it. She needed a friendly smile and a hug. Instead, she got a thoughtless husband, who pointed out something that she really didn't need nor want to hear.

That she was ornery!

Otter Lesson # 3
Otters Don't Criticize Each Other

When faced with a challenge, a bevy of otters all work together to solve it.

The mother and father otters lead, while the older siblings assist. Even the new born pups help. They each do as much as they can, given their personal abilities, to meet the needs of the group.

These otters do not criticize each other. Nor do they find fault in the weaknesses of a fellow den mate. Each otter simply does his or her best to contribute whatever they are able.

Because they do not criticize each other, they are all able to live in harmony with one another.

On that same note, male otters don't see it as their personal responsibility to solve all of the other otter's problems.

Granted, otters can't talk. However the comparison is still valid!

For whatever reason, we men like to solve problems. It is in our blood. We just really struggle with the notion that it is not our job to help others overcome whatever challenges that they might encounter. When we see a problem, we just naturally go into problem solving mode!

When our wives have a bad day, we want to fix it for them. If we are going to help make their day better, then we feel like we have to fully understand the root causes of their bad day. This prompts us to ask foolish questions, like "honey, why are your so ornery?"

Rather than sounding helpful or concerned to our wives, we instead come off as critical, and usually end up making things worse.

If we only occasionally strive to "help" our wives improve their attitudes then they will probably forgive us.

The real issue arises when we persistently and regularly point out their problems.

Our wives don't want to hear about all of their shortcomings all of the time! No one would want to hear that!

If we repeatedly harp on our dear companions over a long period of time, or if our comments relate to something that they already feel self-conscious about, like their weight, then our words will become downright cruel and feel especially devastating.

Your wife has flaws. She has things that you could criticize her for if you so desired.

I know that you loved and admired your sweetheart on the day that you were married. You probably thought that she was perfect in every single way. But guess what! She isn't!!

You will undoubtedly discover as the years roll along that she actually does have a weakness or two tucked away somewhere.

I am sure that even Eve had a few irritating quirks that drove Adam crazy!!

When you married her, did you expect her to never make any mistakes? Were you under the impression that she would never be ornery, never get depressed, never gain weight, or that she would never do anything thoughtless.

43

If you thought that she was going to be perfect, then I am sorry to inform you that you were mistaken.

When she has a bad day, it is your job to quietly listen to her, and to then open your arms and give her a nice long hug.

Your wife has weaknesses! Accept it, get over it, and move on! It is not your job to solve them, or even to point them out. It is your job to simply love her unconditionally.

After all, she puts up with all of your weaknesses!!

Have you ever stopped to consider how often your wife has overlooked the annoying things that you do?

Like when you snore loudly at night, or when you feed the kids ice cream for dinner. She overlooks when you throw your clothes on the bedroom floor rather than into the hamper like she has asked you to do a thousand times.

She ignores when you forget to make the bed. Or when you stay up late, playing video games. When you raise your voice unnecessarily, forget to kiss her goodbye, or any number of other irritatingly thoughtless things that you do.

Imagine for a moment what your marriage would be like if she tried to solve all of your problems for you! How would you feel if she kept an ongoing list of all your weaknesses and then even worse if she saw it as her personal mission to fix you?

How would it be if every single time you rose your voice just a little louder than was really necessary, she said "Honey are you angry again?"

How would you feel if she criticized your balding head, or your harry back, or the red dots and skin tags that are mysteriously showing up all over your body?

When you see your wife struggling with a moment of weakness, give her a big hug, and then just let it go. She knows she messed up. She doesn't need you to tell her.

Just because you are not being critical of your wife, does not however mean that you can't still have a positive impact on her life or on her personality.

You can!! It is just not accomplished by being critical of her. Instead, you have to identify, focus on, and accentuate her talents.

It is your job to build her up to a sort of mythical status in the eyes of your children, your neighbors, and especially in the eyes of her friends.

Take advantage of very opportunity that you can find to sincerely compliment your wife. When she does something amazing, let the entire world know how passionately you love her for whatever amazing thing that she did.

As you put her on a pedestal, and make her out to be a role model, you will help your wife find her groove. She will grow into, and begin to identify with those personality traits that she already had, but that you helped her accentuate.

Don't make these compliments up. They have to be truthful and absolutely sincere. The foundation of her mythical princess-like status must be built out of reality or it will crumble under her feet. She will see through your insincerity, and in the end it will not be helpful to you or to her.

You can always find something to truly and sincerely praise her for. The more you do so, the greater will be your children's appreciation for their angelic mother. Likewise the more that you brag on her, the greater will be the respect and admiration that your neighbors and friends will have for her!

You will know that you have truly succeeded in your mission, when everyone around you starts to wonder how it is even possible that a man like you EVER talked an amazing woman like her into marrying you!

The world will view your wife by the brush that you use to paint her with. To a large extent, she will also view herself that way!

She was already amazing long before you ever met her. That is why you married her! You are simply helping to educate her, your children, and the world about the phenomenal soul that she is.

My father was a master at this. He taught us as children to understand how wonderful, patient, kind, and smart our mother was. In so doing, he reinforced these traits in her.

They were there to begin with. He didn't create them in her. However by constantly hearing my father speak of how wonderful she was, my mother was able to more surely find her talents, and build on them.

Any weaknesses that my mother may have had, took care of themselves. Though I never heard my father speak of them.

Again, you will be the primary means by which the world judges your wife. You alone can be her biggest advocate or her biggest critic. It will be you who defines her to everyone else, and in large part to herself.

Don't take that responsibility lightly.

Chapter 4

Root For The Success of Your Dear Companion

Personal Story

Often *we don't realize or even notice that the pages of our lives are turning over, and that we are about to begin a new and very different chapter of existence.*

As we go through the motions of living it can seem as though each day is indistinguishable from the hundreds that came before.

When without any prior warning something dramatic occurs, and life completely rearranges itself. We are then left to face new roles, new obligations, and new expectations.

Such a change recently occurred in my home. But before I can share this monumental shift in our family life, first allow me to step back a few years, and give you a little bit of background information.

When I was 21 years old I started an educational company. It seemed like a natural fit for me. I enjoyed working with children and I have a lifelong fascination with science.

So starting an organization that worked to introduce children to science was something that made sense and that came naturally to me.

Because my work was fun, it wasn't hard for me to find the motivation to spend often as many as 18 hours in a single day, working towards advancing the organization that I was building.

What started as a small project steadily grew into a series of products and services that would eventually be used by hundreds of millions of students all over the world.

Our materials were being utilized in school systems on every continent and in virtually every country on Earth.

Throughout this journey, my dear wife Anna remained supportive and always at my side. She sacrificed her own goals and dreams so that I could follow mine, and so that our seven children would be well looked after. Something I will forever be grateful for.

I could not have dedicated the time that it took to build a company, had she not been there as a full time mother.

The success of our company is as much her success as it is mine! We built our family, and our company together! Side by side.

Though we each had a slightly different focus, we accomplished the two objectives unitedly.

I worked very hard to build our business, and then came home and spent time with our kids.

She worked even harder to ensure that our kids got to school on time, got fed, and were well cared for, and then looked over my shoulder and gave her input and feedback regarding our business.

These routines continued month after month, and year after year, until one day it all completely changed.

Our youngest two children, who are twins, had at long last, reached a critical milestone in every parent's life. When they would be away from home for seven hours each day! They had reached the age of six and as a result would both be starting the first grade!

For the first time in 18 years all of our children would be gone during the day. Leaving Anna home alone.

Though she deserved a break, Anna is not the type to sit back and take it easy. She therefor decided that it was time for her to start chasing after some of her own deferred dreams.

Meanwhile, I had grown tired of my company. Building it was a lot of fun. However, running a successful company on autopilot is exceedingly boring. It had long since grown into something far bigger than I had ever dreamed it would.

I felt fulfilled and satisfied.

Taking our company even further interested me less and less with each passing month, and as a result, I was getting neglectful of my duties to its future. Something that I was both well aware of, and also not proud of.

These two colliding moments on both sides of our marriage came together to led us to make a few drastic changes in our lives.

For my part, I found investors willing to purchase a majority stake in my company. I promised to stay on as the President of the company in name, but on the condition that I could turn my heart, time, and energy towards something that I had wanted to do ever since I was in kindergarten.

If you had asked me when I was five years old what I wanted to be when I grew up, I would have told you that I was going to be a teacher. Indeed, if you had asked me that same question at any point in my childhood, even when I was as old as 18, I would have said that I was going to be a teacher.

Yet life had led me into business, rather than into the field where my heart really longed to be. Which was something that I was determined to change.

I worked hard to get myself qualified to teach, and then to find a teaching position. Within a year of finalizing the sale of my company I was working full time as a middle school science teacher, in the Salt Lake area. For the record, I have never been happier. I LOVE IT!

As my wife Anna contemplated which of her goals that she wanted to tackle, she first considered starting her own shoppe where she would sell yarn.

Anna has a real talent for knitting and crocheting, and thought that it might be fun to spend her time helping to teach others to do the same. Something that I would have wholeheartedly supported.

However after a great deal of thought and personal soul searching on her part, she eventually decided that what she really wanted to do was to pursue her own childhood dream of becoming a nurse. In order to make this dream a reality we enrolled my wife in nursing school, and she began her journey towards that end.

Suddenly, our entire world was flipped on its head. I was no longer a businessman. I was a teacher. She was still an amazing mother, but was now also a very good nurse.

Now, with these life changes in mind, consider an important point. Nurses make far more money than do teachers!

The selling of our business allowed us to secure our finances and to establish a safety net beneath us. A safety net that we do not draw on. It is saved as a nest egg for the future.

Meaning that our day to day expenses are now coming from the combined wages of my wife and myself. Two thirds of those wages are the funds that she is earning.

Put another way, my wife makes twice as much money as I do, and is now the primary bread winner in our household!

Otter Lesson # 4
Only A Stupid Otter Refuses Extra Oysters!

A male otter doesn't care whether he or his mate catches the most oysters! The notion is obviously preposterous and absurd. He is grateful for the delicious slimy morsels, regardless of who it was that first found them.

You are not in competition with your wife. You are a team. If she succeeds it is the exact same thing as if it were you who was succeeding.

If she does something well, be there for her! Support her! It is not a slight against you or your manhood that she is better at some things than you are.

Would you really want to be married to a partner who had no talents at all, and who never did anything well? Sure, it would allow you to feel superior, but only a fool would choose feeling superior over being more financially stable!

Whether it is in business, or with regards to making money, or in producing art, or at sports, or with public speaking, or in terms of intellect and intelligence, or in any other sphere or domain of human existence. Don't compete with your wife.

Let her be better than you. It is okay. Root for her, and take great joy in watching her be good at those things in which she excels.

I am not suggesting incidentally that you can't ever beat your wife at anything. You have talents as well! You are better than she is at certain things. Just don't rub your successes in her face. Allow her to root for you, while you do the same for her.

The point is that you not use your own success as an opportunity to demoralize her. Likewise that you not feel demoralized by her successes.

I am not the least bit ashamed that my dear sweetheart makes twice as much money as I do. I am grateful for the extra income! That money benefits me as much as it benefits her! We are a partnership. We succeed or fail together.

Resenting your wife's success will cause you to work against her, rather than supporting and cheering for her. As you do so, you will slowly rob her emotional well being, in order to gratify your own personal pride.

If she is better than you at art, then hang her pictures all over the house and make sure that every guest who visits your home hears you brag about them.

If she is a better racquetball player, then support her by going to her matches and cheering for her. If she is smarter than you, then be grateful that your best friend who you turn to for advice is so wise!

Don't be a stupid otter! Don't refuse extra oysters, just because your mate caught them!

Do all in your power to celebrate, promote, and further your dear wife's successes.

Chapter 5
Make Her Appear To Be Perfect In Every Way

Personal Story

Christmas is an infectious time of year! The decorations, the lights, the traditions, and the many years of warm cozy bottled up memories.

Memories which are frequently brought back to my recollection as I pull out old decorations, or taste tempting Christmas snacks.

One of the Christmas traditions that has been apart of my own Christmas experience ever since I was a baby, and that still continues to this day, is that of eating lunch at my grandmother's house.

Grandma is now a little older, and slightly less agile than she use to be. However at 90 years old she still takes the time to put together an impressive Christmas spread. One that would be worthy of being featured on the cover of a 1950's house keeping magazine.

As one of the very few Christmas traditions that still endures from my childhood, this luncheon is something that I really look forward to.

The same pictures still hang on Grandma's living room walls. The same knickknacks are still on her shelves. She even still serves the food on the same platters!

It was during one of these treasured Christmas lunches a few years ago, that I overheard something that gave me great pause for reflection.

After my father said a blessing on the food, Grandma directed her guests to begin to partake of the wonderful and lovingly prepared meal that she had made.

There were various assorted types of potato chips that were sat out in their usual spots. Vegetables that had been laid out in perfect uniform patterns. As well as a wide

60

selection of dips, salsas, different varieties of cheeses, ham, turkey, and several other tempting snacks that had each been carefully prepared and perfectly presented.

After loading up our plates, and in the process making a jumbled mockery of all of the platters that Grandma had taken so long to fastidiously prepare, we each sat down around the kitchen table and began to converse. The meal was as rich in flavor as it was in warmth, for the memories that it evoked.

After a few minutes of inconsequential conversation, one of Grandma's guests, who had sometime earlier gone through a divorce, expressed her opinion that she believed that it was okay and even helpful for a spouse to complain to their mother about their partner behind his back.

She went on to express her belief that talking about your marriage partner in a negative way with a trusted friend or parent, could even be therapeutic.

Given that several of my children were in the room, and that silence can often be misconstrued as agreement, I felt that it was necessary to speak up.

It was important to me that my children knew that their father would never ever complain about their mother

61

behind her back. Not to my friends, not to my coworkers, nor even to my own parents.

I left no room for anyone who was at that kitchen table to doubt my feelings on the subject. I made it absolutely clear that no one would ever hear me utter a negative word about my dear precious Anna!

I explained to the room at large, though my comments were in reality directed towards my own children, that talking about your spouse behind their back was one of the most destructive things that you could do to your marriage.

Fortunately a cousin then stepped in and wisely changed the subject to a less controversial topic, so that the spirit of the day could be preserved.

Though I risked offense, I felt the risk was worth it. Tiny ears were listening, and watching their dad to see how I would react. Their understanding of how I treat their mother, and ultimately their own worldview were on the line!

Otter Lesson # 5

Otters Are Remarkably Good At Keeping Confidences

Tell an otter a secret. Then sit back and see how long it takes for him to tell someone else. My guess is that he never will.

If you ever need to get a burden off your chest, and want to share it with someone who you can absolutely count on, an otter is a good choice! An otter will never betray the confidences that he is entrusted with.

Your life's partner deserves the same.

I can think of few things more damaging to your relationship than to speak ill of your wife behind her back. Or for that matter, to speak ill of her when she is around, but in the presence of other people.

None of us are perfect, and strong marriages endure across many decades. These two facts taken together mean that it is absolutely inevitable that at some point your wife is going to say or do something thoughtless, aggravating, or irritating. This reality is an absolute fact. Something that you can count on happening.

It doesn't matter who you are married to, or how sweet or talented she may be. There will come a moment when she is tired, cranky, forgetful, or otherwise unfair in her treatment of you.

Knowing that this moment is going to inevitably come, you are unwise if you do not prepare yourself for it in advance. How are you going to react? Are you going to get spiteful and attempt to ruin her reputation?

Are you going to be so unwise and so small minded as to share her shortcomings with someone else? Are you going to use her mistake as an excuse to seek out sympathy from a third party?

Are you really going to undermine your efforts to convince the world that she is an angel who stands on a pedestal and who is worthy of adoration, just because she made an inevitable mistake?

It is easy to convince ourselves that we are justified in posting a cryptic message on social media, or in complaining to a parent or friend. We tell ourselves that all we are doing is venting, or that we are just seeking advice.

The reality is that what we are really seeking is for someone to validate our anger, and to justify our offense.

You ought to be aware that these efforts generally reflect more negatively upon yourself than they do on your companion. People see through your cryptic postings, and tend to lose respect for you.

The damage that you do to the trust that she had in you will be difficult to repair.

By betraying her reputation and speaking ill of your wife behind her back, you will leave her brokenhearted, confused, and unlikely to confide in you for a very long time.

Never ever under any circumstances speak badly of your wife to any other person. She needs to know that she can count on you to always make her look and sound good to others.

Even if your negative comments are made in confidence and under circumstances where you think that she will never find out, you will still have violated her trust, and betrayed your duty to her.

I am not suggesting that when these inevitable moments arise where your wife does do something bothersome to you, that you can't ever communicate this to her. She loves you, and she wants to please you. It is always okay to communicate how you feel.

So long as you do so in private, and in a calm non-accusatory manner, when no one else is around, and when no one else can hear you. If you have an issue, it is between you and her. It is your own private business. No one else should ever know that any such issues existed!

As far as anyone else knows, your marriage is absolutely perfect in every single way.

Take her out to dinner, and during the course of the evening say something like "You know what honey I really love you. I know you love me too, and I am so grateful for all you do! Sometimes you do something that bothers me. It is a silly little thing really, and I know it shouldn't bother me. I am actually probably to blame for being so easily annoyed, but I wanted to let you know that when you…" Then follow up again with how much you love her.

You have communicated your irritation to her, in a loving and kind way. She now knows how you feel, and because she loves you, she will try to respect your feelings. She may still do the irritating thing again in the future. Changing old habits is hard, so be patient.

Earlier I suggested that you should never ever under any circumstances speak negatively about your wife. Whether it be behind her back, or in her presence when someone else is also near enough to hear.

Does this mean that you can't seek out guidance or advice from a friend, a counselor, a parent, or a trusted member of your local clergy?

The answer is twofold. Firstly, of course it is okay to seek advice from those whom you trust. Just ask her permission first, and then secondly bring her along with you!

As you seek counsel and advice, never put your wife down. You are a companionship. Own the problem together. Don't say "my wife is doing this wrong...," instead say "we are doing this wrong."

If someone asks how your wife is doing, your answer is always that she is perfect. She is perfect in every single way! You tell them that you can't believe how lucky you are that she is your wife. Let them know that you feel like you must have won the wife lottery, and that as a reward they gave you the absolute best woman who has ever walked the face of the Earth.

Whether you are speaking to your parents, her parents, your siblings, your friends, or a random stranger on the subway. Never share the smallest irritating detail about her to anyone else.

Chapter 6

It Isn't A Bevy Unless There Are Baby Otters

Personal Story

"DADDY!!!"

The shrill voice of my three year old daughter reverberated from off of the living room walls, as my sweet little baby girl dropped her toys, jumped up onto her feet, and began running towards me with her tiny little arms thrown open as widely as she could stretch them.

It had been a very long day, and I was tired. Due to a variety of challenges at work I had reached the very limits of my patience and energy. I needed time to decompress, and gather my thoughts together.

The fact that I was tired didn't however matter in the least to my three year old daughter. She didn't understand how tough my day had been. She didn't even know that the man who she called "Daddy" was capable of being tired. Nor did she know that there were such things as bad days.

All that my daughter knew was that she hadn't seen me all day, and that at last, I had finally walked through the door.

I knelt down, extended my arms outward, and was hit in the chest by a toddler running full speed, on a mission to cuddle with someone who she knew loved her.

As we both fell backwards together onto the floor and as I kissed her soft little baby cheeks, somehow the trials of the day no longer mattered. They became irrelevant. My baby girl had brought everything back into its proper perspective.

The hardships and challenges of work went from being my primary focus, to just being small obstacles that existed somewhere in the background, but that truly did not have any real impact on my life, or level of happiness.

70

I was reminded in a literal flash that I am a father and husband first and foremost. Everything else that I am or that I do is secondary, and derives its importance only from how much it does or does not enable me to support my family.

The stresses that I felt at work were indeed real. The deadlines that had been imposed upon me all had to be adequately satisfied. As an honorable man I knew that I had an absolute obligation to fulfill my commitments outside of my home as best as I was physically able to.

However my roles and titles outside of my home could not ever be allowed to define how I viewed myself. I knew that if I defined myself as a businessman, a teacher, or whatever other title I might have, then I would be missing the entire point of life.

In that moment, the tiny little arms that were tightly grasping my neck made it immeasurably clear to me that the real source of accomplishment in my life would always be my family.

Little kisses from toddlers are far more satisfying than ANY accolade, successful meeting, or any other achievement outside of the home.

71

Likewise any stress, any perceived failure, any bad meeting, or any missed opportunity, can all be wiped away in an instant and made utterly irrelevant by walking into your successfully run home.

In that moment I knew that I could never be a failure, as long as this little munchkin grew up to be a well cared for and successful adult.

She and her siblings were the definition of my success as a man. Not anything that the world might attempt to label me with, or define me by.

Otter Lesson # 6

An Otter's Primary Purpose Is To Bring Forth And Prepare The Next Generation of Otters

---

After selecting their lifelong companions, the first thing that otters do is to procreate. Indeed, this is the very act that signifies that they have formed a lifelong union with each other

Sea otters don't put off having children until after they have attend Otter University. Nor do they wait until after they have conquered the best territory. They don't say to each other that they will first stockpile a lifetime supply of oysters in the bank and then have babies. Nor do they take time to travel the oceans and see the world before bringing pups into their bevy.

They begin to reproduce the very moment that they select each other as companions. Absolutely nothing comes before their starting of their family.

These otters then work closely with their offspring. They spend upwards of two years teaching them how to hunt, how to use rocks to open clam shells, as well as everything else that a baby otter needs to know in order to one day survive on its own in the wild as an adult otter.

Just as it is an otter's primary function to reproduce, and to dedicate their time and energy to raising successful offspring, so to is it your primary function to be a father.

The purpose of this book, as stated from the outset, is to act as a guidebook and to lead you towards a life of joy and happiness.

When it comes to feeling a fullness of absolute joy and boundless happiness, the following point cannot be overstated.

You will never reach your full capacity for happiness unless you fulfill your obligation to become a father and tenderly care for and love your offspring.

I have known people who have believed otherwise. Who thought that it all came down to personal preference. These individuals believed that they could choose to avoid having children, and instead spend their time and money on themselves, and on their own private pursuits.

They further unwisely believed that the happiness that they felt in their childless life was the maximum amount of joy that any other human being felt.

As every parent who has ever lived will readily testify, these individuals couldn't be more wrong!

I will not attempt to argue whether or not they may be experiencing some level of happiness. But they have denied themselves access to the greatest source of joy that is available to a man.

Until you become a parent yourself, there exists no place in your heart to fully comprehend the meaning of these words.

You can try to understand them on an intellectual level. However you will never even get close to comprehending the emotional impact that your little ones will have on your heart and life until the doctor places that tiny little ball of wrinkles into your arms, and you suddenly realize that your life will never again be the same.

When a man chooses to avoid being a father, he robs himself of life's most choicest blessings. Nothing you do will ever have as big of an emotional impact on you.

Hearing your three year old daughter screech "DADDY," is an unbelievably awesome thing!   There are no words in the English language so powerful as the word daddy when it has been spoken by one of your little ones.

It will melt your heart, change your life, and bring you to a state of nirvana that is utterly inexpressible and impossible to adequately describe.

I am blessed to be the father of four beautiful daughters, as well as three honorable sons. Just as my precious little girls melt my heart, so to do my sons have a profound impact on my personal psyche.

My three sons look up to their dad. I can see it in their eyes. They have great respect for my counsel, and see me as someone who they can trust. It is important to them that I be proud of them. As a result they want and actively seek out my approval.

The weight of such a deep level of absolute trust and admiration is tremendous! I stand in awe of it.

That I am that important, and that looked up to by these three boys weighs ever present in my mind. It is one of the greatest privileges of my life to be so loved and so respected.

Whether you deserve it or not, your daughters will adore you and long for your attention. Your sons will admire you, and seek your approval. This profound love and abiding respect are wonderful. However this adoration will not be the greatest source of joy that you will find in parenting.

Rather the greatest joy that you will find in fatherhood will come as a result of how effectively you are able to utilize and leverage the love and respect that your children have for you, in order to bring about each of their own long term well being, and as result prepare them for adulthood.

Because they trust you, they will come to you when they have problems. Occasionally they may even consider actually following your advice. Which puts you into a position to give well placed counsel from time to time that will establish them on the road towards a happy and successful life of their own.

Seeing your children grow into their own, becoming dependable, functional, and independent adults will bring you tremendous pride. To get to observe them as they advance from childhood towards adulthood, and to watch them make good choices will provide an endless source of joy for you.

This pride will be far more precious to you than any fortune, any promotion, any vacation, or any other worldly thing that you might have achieved or accomplished outside of your home.

I want to end this chapter by reiterating one of the most important points that is made in this book. Which is that you will never feel like a failure, if you are successful in your home.

Even on your darkest days, when you get laid off from work, or your business fails, or you have to declare bankruptcy, or your house gets repossessed, or any other measure by which the world declares you to have failed.

The sting of that moment will be real, but it will also be short lived, and ultimately non-consequential to your own sense of peace and self-confidence.

These so-called failures will look and feel utterly insignificant to you when compared to your success as a father.

When you contemplate the course of your life, you will feel no regrets if you have been an effective father.

You will know that while you perhaps didn't accomplish everything that you had dreamed or hoped that you would in terms of wealth and fame, that you were nevertheless an absolute success in those things that mattered most.

A very wise man once said that "No other success in life can compensate for failure in the home.[3]" The reverse of this famous quote is equally true. No failure in the world

---

3   David O. McKay

can take away from or diminish your successes in your home!

The sooner that you start your family the sooner that you can open the door to life's greatest source of personal fulfillment.

Putting fatherhood off or opting out of it entirely so that you can pursue some worldly experience or achieve a meaningless temporal goal only delays or destroys what would have been your single greatest achievements.

Chapter 7

Raising Children Is Far Less Expensive Than You Might Think

Personal Story

"Can you believe how ridiculous these claims are!"
I stated with righteous indignation to no one in particular.

My grumpy old man skepticism dripped down my expressions. "Where on Earth do they come up with this nonsense!"

My wife Anna put down her book, smiled softly and looked up at me.

While imperceptibly rolling her eyes, and sighing quietly to herself Anna made an expression that suggested that she loved me enough to fain interest in whatever it was that I was so irritated by this time.

Though she was only mildly amused, and mostly annoyed that I was interrupting what she was reading, she didn't say this out loud. Instead, her words were kind and genuinely inquisitive.

After taking a moment to check her voice and expressions, she asked me in a tone that sounded sincere. As though she really did care, "What is wrong sweetheart?"

Even though I knew full well that Anna was only humoring me, I nevertheless couldn't let it go. Not until I had adequately vented my disagreement with an online source that I had never before met, and who would never actually hear how ardently I disagreed with them.

I suppose that I believed that if I spoke my disagreements out loud that they would somehow magically float across the room, out of the window, and then fly directly towards the idiot who wrote the article that I was reading. Slapping that person in the face, and informing them of how stupid they were.

The article that had so incensed me related to the cost of raising children. It had appeared in my news reader, along with several other similar stories that were showing up on the same day and on the same topic.

All of these stories had been prompted by a press release from The United States Department of Agriculture, which had tried to quantify how much money it costs parents to raise a child from birth to the age of 18. This organization concluded that in would cost the parents of a child born today some $245,340 to raise their son or daughter to adulthood[4].

After reading Anna the article, I pulled out my smart phone and opened the calculator app. I then sarcastically continued my contemptuous diatribe. "This means that according to the Department of Agriculture, it should cost you and I $1.7 million to raise our family!!"

I looked over at my patient wife, who now wore an expression that looked like "That's nice dear." Though she didn't say it out loud.

---

4   http://blogs.usda.gov/2014/08/18/how-much-will-it-cost-to-raise-a-child/

"Do you realize that with that much money I could not only buy each one of our children their own home, but I could also pay for their entire childhood, as well as the childhoods of all our grandchildren!!"

"With that much money I could make sure that all seven of our kids had a comfortable roof over the heads, completely paid off, and that none of them ever had to work!"

I shook my head, and looked back down at my tablet. Anna looked at me sweetly, waited a moment to make sure that I was done, then detecting that I had stepped down from off my soapbox went back to her book.

I had said my peace and had released my opinions into the air. Leaving me feeling better, and able to again focus on reading the rest of the news stories of the day.

Otter Lesson # 7

Otters Don't Have Any Money! Yet Somehow They Thrive.

No matter how long you watch them play, swim, hunt, or just lounge about, I promise you that you will never ever see an otter pull out his ATM card. Nor will you hear him or her talk about how much raising their baby otters costs.

They are poorer than the lowliest vagabond. Yet despite this fact, these otters somehow manage to not only survive, but to thrive.

As humans, we can't avoid the reality that money matters. We have to have an income. Our circumstances are different from those of a family of otters in obvious and important ways.

Regardless, this otter lesson is still valuable and one worth pondering. Just as is the case with otters, most of the things that constitutes a comfortable and secure life for us, are totally free. But again, not everything is free.

A second category of things that we need in order to raise our families are those things that do have a financial cost associated with them.

However as you will see that many of these costs do not increase or compound as additional family members are added into your household.

There are however some that do. A few of the expenses that we are responsible for as parents absolutely will increase with each individual who we add to our families. Fortunately these expenses that are usually not very high, and if carefully managed can have their impact dramatically lessened.

Firstly, let's talk briefly about the things that really matter in life. The things that are free, and that will largely constitute what your kids will remember about their childhood years from now.

When they are older, and they think back on their time in your home, your children are not going to think about how big their home or apartment was. They are not going to remember any car troubles that you may have had. Nor are they likely to think about any other physical things having to do with wealth.

What they will recall with fondness is the quality time that you spent with them. The traditions that you shared together. The camping trips that you took. The times when you set down everything that you were doing, went on a walk with them, and listened to their problems.

They will remember the hikes that you took them on. Playing at the park, exploring the neighborhood, the pets that you kept, and a million other little things that cost you little or no money.

The tender richness of their childhood memories will have nothing whatsoever to do with how much money you made.

It will have everything to do with how you loved them, and how much time you spent with them.

This being said, it is nevertheless still important to care for their needs and to provide for them. Indeed as a father, you have an absolute responsibility to make sure that your children's needs are met.

I don't minimize these obligations. However you need to understand that as long as these basic needs are satisfied then they will barely even live in their memories. What they will care about and treasure are your time and your love. These are the things that will make their lives sweet, and their memories tender.

These are the things that will most define your success as a parent, and that will have the greatest impact on their well being.

While the most important and influential things in life are 100% free of charge, there are still undeniable and unavoidable costs associated with raising children.

Let's spend a few moments talking about the two categories of expenses that remain. Firstly those things whose costs do not increase with the number of members in your household, followed by a brief discussion of those things whose costs do compound.

You will find that most of the expenses that are associated with raising a family either do not increase or do not increase very much as the number of individuals who live in your household rises. These are costs that you likely would have had even as a single individual.

I mentioned earlier that you have a responsibility to provide a home for your children. Whether you have two children, five children, or eight, the cost associated with finding and maintaining a home does not dramatically increase.

True, you many need a larger home with a few extra bedrooms, but the difference in cost between a 2 bedroom home and a four bedroom home is honestly not that great.

Especially if you are willing to work a few extra weekends on your own home improvement projects. Consider purchasing a two bedroom home with an unfinished basement, and then building a couple of extra bedrooms yourself. Or just buy bunk beds. The kids will have fond memories of when they shared bedrooms.

The home that my wife and I live in is one that we had had our eye on for 15 years prior to purchasing it. It is a local home that we really liked. Both in terms of style and location. When it finally went up for sale, we purchased it.

If Anna and I had been childless we would still have purchased the same home that we currently inhabit.

Therefore this cost can be entirely discounted as it relates to raising our kids. The same goes for you. Whether you have kids or not, you are going to have to live somewhere.

Would the cost that you pay for a house filled with children really be increased all that much over what you would pay for a home that didn't have any kids in it? I suspect that what you currently pay in rent or on your mortgage wouldn't go up by very much, just by adding a single baby into your family.

The amount that the Department of Agriculture suggests that it costs parents to provide a home for each of their children is $73,000 per child! For that much money I could build each one of my kids their own private cottage.

The real cost per child is somewhere closer to $0 to perhaps as much as $10,000 depending on your own personal circumstances, and after considering how you choose to live both before and after having children.

Many other categories of expenses that are included in the Department of Agriculture's estimate for raising a child are likewise not compounded by the number of individuals in a household.

In most cases there is no increased transportation cost with each child that you add to your family. The car is already driving to school. Regardless of how many little bodies climb inside of it.

Yet the US Department of agriculture estimates the cost of transporting each child at over $34,000 per child. I could buy each of my children their own personal high-end SUV, and still have money left over to pay for the gas to drive each one individually.

If you live in a place where you utilize public transportation then there is going to be a deferred increase in individual costs per child. However, even a lifetime supply of bus passes would never come close to the $34,000 estimated price tag given in this report.

I would also loosely fit clothing into the category of expenses that are not compounded. To be fair the cost of clothes does increase with each child. However not by very much.

Kids grow up very quickly. They rarely use the same size outfits long enough to wear them out. Making these perfectly good clothes perfectly available to be worn by the next child down, and then even the child after that.

Furthermore in today's world, with the ready availability of discount department stores, second hand shops, and generous neighbors, the cost of clothing is not that high to begin with.

I recently purchased school clothes for all seven of my children. We went to a local department store, and I turned them loose. I told each child that they had $100 to spend, and that they had to get a certain number of shirts, pants, underwear, and socks. After several minutes we regrouped. Each child had stayed within their budget and came away very happy.

I will not claim that $700 isn't a lot of money, It is! However keep in mind that this one time per year expense was for seven children. If you have two children, then your actual cost would be closer to $200 per year.

After shopping for school clothes, I took my kids home, and together we went through the mountain of clothes that we have collected over the years.

Everyone brought all their clothing down to the living room, so that we could see what each one had, and what kind of shape it was in. Things were divided and redistributed based on size, and then returned to bedrooms accordingly.

Every child had outfits and to spare. This included items that they had personally selected and purchased, as well as plenty of hand-me-downs. Leaving them with

92

enough outfits so that they never would have to wear the same thing twice in a week, or even in a month.

Moreover, there are always people in your neighborhood getting rid of clothes. We have had multiple family members and friends stop by over the years with a bag full of clothes asking us if we wanted any of it.

The US Department of Agriculture suggests that it will cost you as a parent more than $14,000 to clothe each of your children during the first 18 years of their lives.

What are these parents buying their kids, in order to spend that much money on clothing!! This would come out to just under $800 a year per child, or put another way, more money than the amount that my wife and I spend on all seven of our children combined.

If we spent $14,000 per child on clothes, then in our family that would come out to a grand total of $98,000! Enough clothing to easily fill every room in our entire house from floor to ceiling!

Most of the expenses that you will incur as a parent do not compound as the number of children increases. However some do.

Let's now briefly talk about this third category that I mentioned. Those expenses which will unavoidably increase as you bring more children into your family.

The biggest expense that immediately comes to mind is that of food. As the number of mouths in your home increases, and as they each grow older, your grocery bill is going to unavoidably increase.

The US Department of Agriculture estimates that as a parent you will pay $40,000 per child over the course of their 18 years in your care in order to feed them. This comes out to $185 per month, per child.

According to these numbers, my wife and I should be spending something like $1,300 a month on groceries, for just our children, and not even taking into account the food that she and I eat.

How much do we actually spend? With two adults, three hungry teenagers, two tweens, and two six year olds, our actual grocery bill hovers somewhere between $200 - $400 a month to feed all nine of us. This includes cleaning supplies, toilet paper, shampoo, etc.

I don't even know how to spend $1,300 a month on groceries! What do you buy each month and how can you possibly eat that much food!

In the interest of honesty and fairness, Anna and I do live on a small three acre farm. Though we only use less than half of an acre of that property to produce anything. Most of our property is grass. It is just room for our kids to run and play.

We do have a small garden, a handful of fruit trees, and an old barn where we have from time to time raised a pig, or some other meat providing animal.

Our garden is about 75 feet long, and 40 feet wide. From this small patch of dirt we get enough vegetables to feed our family for the entire year. The reality is that this small garden produces so much produce that 75% of it goes to waste. We could easily feed many more people off of the food that it grows.

Our fruit trees supply us with an impressive amount of apples, peaches, apricots, cherries, pears, and plums. Which we preserve in mason jars, and then save in the garage.

We have two large chest freezers full of meat, that we have raised or purchased from local ranchers, and have had butchered, or in some cases even butchered ourselves.

The result is that all we really buy each month is milk, flour, eggs, sugar, and other basic necessities.

You may be saying to yourself, that our costs are lower because we cheat! And that it is not fair for me to suggest that the cost of groceries that we spend is a realistic cost for everyone else.

My answer to you is that of course we cheat! And so should you. What is stopping your from planting a garden?

It is easy to plant a garden, and it requires very little dirt. Doing so costs less than $100 in the spring, and takes no more than 30 minutes a week to care for.

Fruit trees are another great way to produce lots of free food for your family. They cost a bit more initially, but once they are established fruit trees will keep providing food for your family for decades, with very little care or attention on your part.

Would you call an otter a "cheater" because he catches his own fish rather then buying them at the grocery store?

Like an otter, you can live very comfortably, utilizing those resources that exist all around you. You don't need a lot of money to provide for your little ones. Far less than many would have you believe.

Bring your children into the world with full confidence that you will be able to provide for them. As long as you are willing to work hard, and take the the time required to plant a garden, or to pick the fruit from a tree, or implement whatever other creative solutions that you and your wife come up with together.

Don't be deterred by nonsensical claims that it is too expensive to start a family. These sensational claims are not based in reality.

Chapter 8
Take The Time To Both Bond And To
Encourage Bonding

Personal Story

It was in every way an idealistically perfect moment. An assortment of light green leafs fluttered quietly against the deep blue sky above me. From the perspective of where I laid underneath an old ash tree, I could see a handful of puffy white clouds floating slowly across the sky. The day was warm and bright. A quiet wind gently brushed the surface of my face.

It was the kind of moment where you stop and say "Lord, this moment! This one right here! Let me remember it forever!!"

The colors, the temperature, and the sensation of the breeze against my skin were all pleasant and wonderful! They fed my senses with just the right balance and ambiance.

However the joy of these feelings all paled in comparison to the sensations being delivered by my ears.

As I laid there gazing upward, I could hear off in the distance my seven children splashing and playing together as they ran around our yard.

It was irrigation day! An event that comes once a week during the summer. On irrigation day, we have access to secondary water from a local lake. It makes its way to our yard via a series of canals and ditches. Once there, we use it to flood the entire yard with three to four inches of water.

The kids all inevitably don their swimming attire and go outside to splash, play, catch the random fish that might end up on the lawn, and to enjoy each others company.

Every so often one of my children would run over to the elevated spot where I was laying and flop down on top of me. They would say something like "Dad, I love you."

Or not say anything at all, but instead just lay at my side for a few moments. Before jumping up and flying off again in some random direction, in order to rejoin the fun that the other kids were having running through the water that covered our yard.

My job was easy. I had to monitor the water, to make sure that it didn't flood the basement, and then just be there. Be available to offer on demand snuggles, whenever one of them felt the random desire to be reassured that they were loved and that they were an important part of our family.

Otter Lesson # 8

When They Are Not Busy, Otters Can Almost Always Be Found Snuggling!

The propensity that otters have towards expressing their love for each other is the primary reason that otters are easily my favorite animal.

They adore snuggling. They do so unabashedly, and without any shame or embarrassment.

Otters willingly and regularly both seek out, and offer comfort to and from each other in the form of physical contact.

One evening after returning home from a date that my wife and I had spent alone together, we walked into the house and up to the living room where we found something that brought great joy to both of our hearts.

The five children who had up to that point already been born, were all lying together under a blanket, watching a movie. They expressed no embarrassment in their being discovered snuggling together.

Their arms, legs, and heads were twisted up and poking out from random places underneath the edges of the blanket. Making it difficult for us to distinguish which appendages belonged to which children. They were content and happy to just be close to one another, watching their show.

In a family, this kind of closeness is a top down affair. Meaning that it has to be taught to them from their parents, beginning in their infancy.

The only way that your children are going to learn that snuggling is okay, is if you as their father hold them in your arms beginning on the day that they are first born, and then continue doing so ever after. Hold them often and close.

From the time that they join your home as tiny babies, you should be putting your nose up next to theirs, and giving them little Eskimo kisses. Or pressing your lips against their adorably soft little cheeks.

One thing that I personally enjoy doing is staring into my children's eyes as our foreheads touch, and then pointing out that to me it looks like they only have one eye. I then accuse them of being a cyclopes, which makes them giggle.

Another thing that I like doing is giving my children "cactus kisses." Which mostly involves rubbing my whiskered face against their cheeks.

In addition to being affectionate, it is important that you are also playful.

103

Children have a built in radar for when dad is in a playful mood. They absolutely love taking advantage of these moments.

Try an experiment. Quietly lay down in the middle of your living room carpet. Don't tell anyone in advance that you are doing so.

Once there, start to count how long it takes for one of your kids to discover that you are on the floor. Usually they will find you in less than a minute! The first kid who walks past the door, and notices you will invariably scream, and run full steam towards you.

Once discovered, your job is to then catch their legs, and not let them go. In our house, we call this a snuggle trap.

Just be warned that once you start this game, it takes a really long time for your kids to get bored of it. They will want to keep playing long after you have run out of energy.

After catching their feet, they will try to get away. If they do escape, they will then run back, and try to jump over you again and again.

Trust me, they really do not want to get away! What they want is to be close to you. They only want you to think that they are trying to get away.

After pulling them into the snuggle trap, I might tell them that I am going to "squeeze them back to a baby," because they are growing way too fast.

Alternatively I might hold my hand above one of my children like it is a spider dangling from a spider web. I will then slowly bring my hand down until it lands on their bellies, where I then begin to tickle them.

They scream with delight, squirm wildly in every direction, and beg to be let go. If however you actually do let go of them, they don't run away. No matter how much they protest being stuck in your arms, as soon as you release them, they will say "Catch me again Dad!!"

Another "game" I like to play is to lay on the floor with my belly facing downward, and my back facing up towards the ceiling. Again, I don't give my kids any advance notice. I simply lay there and wait to be discovered. The first kid to find me will run over, and start walking up my legs, across my back, and then jump off over my head. They love walking on my back, and honestly, it makes for a really great free massage!

Children don't know that some people feel uncomfortable holding their parent's hand in the store. This is a learned behavior.

If you start when they are babies, and teach them that it is okay to put their face up next to yours, then when they are older, they will not think twice about whispering a secret into your ear, or grabbing your cheeks and squishing your mouth up into a funny face while you are trying to watch television.

Indeed, if you teach them that showing affection is a normal part of being human, then they will show that affection freely.

More importantly, as a result of being so constantly reassured of your love for them your children will be stronger and more well adjusted in the world.

It is not just them who will draw strength from you. You will also draw strength from their little hugs and kisses, and your own sense of well being will be greatly enhanced, as the result of taking the time to be a good daddy.

Being affectionate and playful are both critical to successful parenting. Additionally, you have to be willing to take individual time with each child, on their own terms.

This means setting down whatever you are doing, when one of your children needs you, and listening to that tiny little person who is trying so desperately to get their daddy's attention.

You are after all, the only daddy that your children have! If you won't listen to them, then they have no other daddy to turn to for help!

Just as children have a natural radar for detecting when you are lying on the floor, they also seem to have a habit of wanting your attention when you are busy doing something important.

They will rarely want to talk during those moments that you plan or set aside to talk to them. Such as on a car ride, or at some other time when your mind and time are not otherwise engaged.

That would be too easy!

Instead they will come up to you when you are deep in thought, working in the zone on something that you really need to finish.

In these moments, it takes tremendous discipline to remind yourself that your children really are more important to you than anything else.

Though difficult, it is worth digging deep in order to find the patience necessary to put everything else down that you were so intently concentrating on, so that you can turn your full attention towards your little ones.

Usually they just want to tell you something that to you may seem unimportant. Such as how they colored stripes on their favorite pony, even though she is supposed to have dots. However sometimes, especially as they get older, they will want to talk about bigger issues that are more important to you as their father.

Moreover what seem like small things to us as adults, can be really difficult and troubling to them as children. After all, they lack the experience and perspective that we have.

As a result of their limited perspective, it takes far less to worry and stress a child, than it does to disquiet an adult.

We make a mistake if we think that a problem that one of our children is struggling with is silly, and therefor should be easy for them to deal with.

Allow me to clarify what I mean, by sharing a somewhat unrelated example.

Remember when you were in the second grade, and for the first time in your life you had to learn to compose entire sentences.

How hard was it for you to write an entire paragraph? Your little hand still struggled to hold a pencil properly. The laborious task of writing so many words down on a piece of paper seemed daunting to your little heart!

Years later when we arrived in middle school was it still difficult for you to write a single paragraph? Of course not! You were now much older, and had had far more experience and practice.

Holding a pencil was now second nature to you. You didn't even give it any thought. You could likewise easily form words and write them down without any trouble at all.

While writing a paragraph was a task that you could now easily accomplish with little effort, do you remember how much it stressed you out when your 7th grade English teacher asked you to write a three page research paper!

You had to learn to cite references, to write an outline, to carry a thought across three entire pages, and to support that thought with evidence. You had to write an introduction, and a conclusion and you had to meet all of the criteria that you teacher had laid out for you, so that you would get a good grade.

Do you remember the late nights and the tears that came from having to write that three page paper!

Now fast forward a few more years to college. How easy would it be for a doctorate student who just finished researching and writing their 300 page dissertation to write a three page middle school essay?

It is all perspective!

Just because a doctorate student could sit down and write a single paragraph in 45 seconds, does not discount the reality of how difficult that same paragraph would be for a seven year old child to write.

It would be unfair of you as a parent to discount the seven year old's frustration, based on the abilities of the college student.

It is likewise unfair of you to discount how upset your seven year old is about their sandwich not being cut properly, based solely on the fact that such a silly thing would never upset an adult.

I am not suggesting that you should coddle your child. Nor that you should allow them to display inappropriate behavior. If they are throwing a fit over a sandwich that has not been cut the way that they like, then you have a duty as a father to correct them.

It is all in how you approach it. Understand that to your child, it truly is a really big deal. At that moment it may very well feel like more than they are able to emotionally handle.

They need to be taught. Just as your second grade teacher helped you learn to hold your pencil correctly.

Take the time to calmly explain why they are going to eat the sandwich even though it was cut wrong. They may still be upset, but at least you have validated their genuine struggle, rather than dismissing it as foolishness.

Likewise, when your 12 year old daughter comes to you upset about how her friend Becky talked more to her other friend Jill, and even though they are both still talking to your daughter, she believes that they left her out, and that they now like each other more than they like her... sigh...,

Don't roll your eyes and dismiss her feelings, based on the irrelevant fact that as an adult male, you couldn't care less what your office companions think of you. Nor do you ever keep track of how often they speak to each other, or whether or not they like one another more than they like you.

Stop, and listen to her. She is hurting. Her feelings are sincere, and of monumental significance to her. She doesn't have the perspective that you do. Which is why you are her dad. Listen to her. Talk with her, and reassure her gently that it will be okay.

As your children become teenagers, they will begin to face increasingly difficult issues that for you as a parent will eventually reach levels that are frightening. Problems such as depression, suicidal thoughts, drugs, and sexuality.

They are not going to bring these problems to you, nor come to you for advice, unless you were there for them years earlier when they needed someone to put the head back on their favorite barbie. Having wiped away those long distant tears. They have to know that you will validate and help, not belittle and diminish their problems.

Listen to your children whenever they want to talk. Take their problems seriously. Validate their struggles, and gently offer wise insights based on your broader perspective.

Now, let's change topics for a moment, and talk about one more important responsibility that you as a father have, that will generate love and closeness within your home.

That is the importance of family vacations and family traditions.

Several years ago while laying in bed one night, I attempted to review and remember every aspect of my entire life. I purposely tried to recall every single event that I could think of. Starting as young as I could remember and then continuing on through the present day.

I went year by year in my mind, trying to think about every location that I had ever been and every single thing that I had ever done.

After coming to the end of this exercise, something interesting occurred to me. Though I had not done so intentionally, the things I had thought about, as I tried to remember everything, were the family vacations that I had been on, and the family traditions that I had participated in. Those are the things that had been important enough for my brain to store them in long term memory.

As I observe my own children, I see the very same thing occurring.

My son said to me the other day "Dad, do you remember when we went to Yellowstone, and saw the bison?" What he didn't say was "Dad, do you remember when we went to the grocery store, and saw the milk!"

In our family we take a minimum of one vacation per year. Depending on our momentary finances this vacation might be anything as extravagant as flying all nine of us to Disney World, or as simple as camping in the mountains above the valley where we live. Our children honestly don't care where we go. They get just as excited to camp in the mountains as they do to fly on an airplane.

What matters is that you take the time to build these lasting memories.

114

Speaking of creating memories, don't wait until your children are old enough to clearly remember an experience before taking them on some exciting adventure.

The far distant memories of early childhood are the most magical! They will treasure their fuzzy memory of riding the dumbo elephants at Disneyland when they were three far more than the crystal clear memories of riding space mountain when they were 17.

If you wait until they are old enough to clearly remember every detail of an experience, then you have missed your opportunity to create what would have been some of their favorite memories in adulthood.

As far as traditions go, in our family we have a few that really mean a lot to us as. One of our favorites is a rotating date night, where two of our children get to go to dinner with mom and dad.

Other traditions include going to the State Fair each year, going downtown on Christmas Eve and walking around the city, walking around the block together on Halloween night, eating Thanksgiving dinner together, swimming outside in a hot spring in the middle of each winter, and a handful of other annual events that our kids know and look forward to.

The magic is in their regularity. Weeks before an event arrives, your children will start to get excited. My six year old son recently counted down the days until we got to go to the State Fair starting when there were still 11 days left. As soon as he woke up each morning he would yell to the entire household "Eight days left until we go to the fair!," or whatever the current count happened to be that day.

The bottom line is that it really doesn't matter what you do. Create whatever traditions that you and your dear sweetheart want. Pick a few things. No more than five or six. Sprinkle them throughout the year, and then remain faithful to them. These will be the events that will live in your children's hearts and memories forever.

Be an otter father!

Be affectionate. Be playful. Take the time to listen. Go on vacations, and create traditions. Your children will benefit tremendously, but the reality is that so to will you.

116

In the quiet moments when you ponder your life's course, you will feel great satisfaction as you think back over the many moments that you have shared with your precious little otters.

These memories will serve as one of the greatest sources of your inextinguishable, ever present, and sometimes irritatingly annoying, unapologetic happiness.

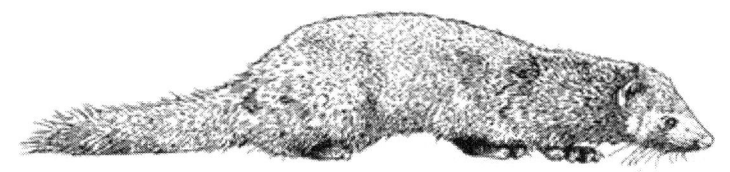

Chapter 9
Teach Them To Share Your Worldview And To Work Hard

Personal Story

"Wake Up!!" I excitedly called throughout the house. "Come on guys! It's time to get up! let's go!"

"Dad! It's early," my oldest daughter grumbled as she attempted to roll over, while pulling her quilt up over the top of her messy hair.

"It's 7:00 am!" I enthusiastically called out to her from across her bedroom. "That isn't early, that is what I like to call late!"

119

"I'll tell you what. I will make you a deal." I continued. "If you don't get up, I will sing the good morning song for you."

"DAAAD! Don't sing!"

"Wake up and say good morning, put on a happy face..."

"DAAAAAD! I AM GETTING UP!"

"Wake up and say how are you..."

"Dad, stop singing!"

"put all your cares a way, GOOD MORNING! Wake up and say good morning, put on a happy face GOOD MORNING, Wake up and say HOW ARE YOU, Put all your cares away, GOOD MORNING!..."

"Your so annoying Dad!"

Outside the air was crisp and cool. However, this brief relief from the summer heat wouldn't last. As the Sun moved higher into the sky, temperatures were supposed to soar to as high as 95 degrees.

My kids were just starting to enjoy their summer vacation. They had undoubtedly envisioned spending a lazy day sleeping in, playing with friends, and then

concluding their day by wasting endless hours on their
electronic devices.

I however had other plans.

I was going to bless their little lives by giving them
the privilege of spending an entire day climbing ladders,
picking, washing, and pitting cherries, and then cooking
and canning jam.

Hooray!! Making jam is WAY more fun than what
they had planned, right!

After waking up each of my seven children with my
beautiful singing, we went outside together to get stated.

"Go grab the buckets out of the garage," I instructed
my younger children. "You two go grab the ladder and the
step stool," I continued as I glanced over at my second and
third children.

After getting everything setup around our cherry
trees, we began the task of filling multiple five gallon
buckets with ripe plump delicious dark red fruit.

It was fun! Or at least I thought it was fun.

As we worked side by side, we chatted about a
thousand different unrelated topics. whatever came to
mind in the moment. I don't recall all the things that we

discussed, but I do recall them asking me why I was so mean and why I was making them all work so hard.

"Anything worth having takes hard work." I cheerfully explained. "If you want to be successful in life, then you can't be afraid to get off of your butt and get to work."

My kids are very used to hearing me talk about work in this manner. It was not the first nor probably the hundredth time that I had shared these lessons with them.

As a result of having spent many days of their childhood working, they have long since given up on complaining about having to work hard. They still mumble and groan, but they don't fall on the floor and refuse to work.

They know that the best thing for them to do is to just bear down, and push through it. If they work fast and hard, then they will finish the job quicker, allowing them to once again regain their freedom.

After three hours of picking cherries, two hours of washing and pitting them, six hours of cooking the cherries down into jam, and then an hour of packing the jam into jars, we sadly ran out of things to do, and had to quit the super exciting task that my kids were "enjoying" so much.

After washing the counters and dishes, we all collapsed into chairs around the kitchen table and rested for a few moments.

As we sat there together covered in the residue of a hundred quarts of jam, I thought about the day and how much I had enjoyed working alongside my kids.

As I pondered our efforts, I silently wondered how they would remember days like this. Would they look back with fondness on the long summer days when their father had gotten them up early, and had stolen all their free time from them, or would they tell their own children "at least I don't make you pick cherries, like my dad did!!".

After a few moments of exhausted though restful quiet, my ten year old son broke the silence by asking, "Dad, can I make a peanut butter and jam sandwich?"

"Me too!!" cried my 14 year old daughter.

Within a few minutes, all seven of my children were back on their feet happily making and eating sandwiches that to them tasted so much sweeter, because of the effort that they themselves had put into making the jam.

As I watched them, I smiled inwardly. Mission accomplished, I thought to myself. I could lecture to them about the value of working hard until I ran out of breathe and passed out on the floor.

However, today, my children had experienced it for themselves. Today they had literally tasted the rewards.

The realization that good things really are worth working hard for was sinking in right in front of my eyes. My children had gained a great sense of pride for their own accomplishments.

Otter Lesson # 9
Adult Otters Teach Young Otters How To Survive In The Wild

My children and I really enjoy watching nature documentaries together. Recently my second youngest daughter and I watched a special about an otter rescue center in Southern California.

This all volunteer run facility cares for otters who have been injured in the wild and who need time and a safe environment in which they can recuperate before they are ready to be released back into the wild. These volunteers also care for otter pups who have been separated from their parents.

While this facility has seen great success in returning adult otters to the ocean, the program emphasized that they really struggle with helping to prepare otter pups to live on their own.

Without proper training, the otters who come to them as pups often die in the wild shortly after being released.

These otters don't understand how to hunt, how to use rocks to pry open clam shells, nor do they have any of the other skills that come naturally to wild otters. Additionally they lack a natural fear of predators, making them easy targets.

These volunteers go to great lengths in order to teach the young otter pups the important survival skills that they will need. However, they readily admit that they make poor substitute teachers for the otters' real parents.

The lesson is clear. No one can adequately fill the shoes of an otter's true parents.

Only the otter's real parents are in a position to train, teach, and guide the baby otters towards adulthood. Likewise no one can fill your shoes as a father.

In your absence others will do the best that they can. They will try to teach, to guide, to love, and to act as a role model. However they will only approximate the success that you would have had. Your role is absolutely critical in the lives of your children.

You can't leave raising your children in the hands of teachers, coaches, neighbors, or friends. Your kids need you to be there. They need you to actively participate in their education, their moral development, and in teaching them how to succeed in the adult world.

What exactly does it mean to teach your children to be successful adults? What are you supposed to teach them? How are you supposed to teach them?

The answers to these questions are going to be different for each individual situation, culture, community, religion, and even for each one of your children.

Each child is unique. Their personalities will require that you customize the lessons that you teach them. Your community, your religion, and your culture are also unique.

It is therefor impossible for me to layout a specific set of lesson plans that you should use in raising your children. Instead, I can only speak generally about what your children will need to know prior to entering the adult world.

However, this much I can say. It is your absolute and unavoidable responsibility to teach your children to follow after and to subscribe to your own personal worldview.

I sometimes hear parents say that they are holding off on teaching their children to believe in their religion until these kids are old enough to choose for themselves. Taking such an approach is a dereliction of your duty as a parent.

When will they be old enough? When they are 10? When they are 15? By then you will have already lost too many of your most effect years of instruction.

Just as it takes a pianist many years to learn to perfectly play one of Scott Joplin's ragtime classics, it likewise takes a child years of practice to learn to be polite, to believe in God, to work hard, or to master whatever other skills and beliefs that you personally believe are important.

If you wait until they ask you to teach them, then chances are very high that they never will ask. Even if they do, by then it will be too late to have as big of an impact on their lives as you might have otherwise had.

To understand how this works, let's consider a quick example.

A young child learns to speak a language almost without effort. By the time that this young child reaches the age of five or six years old, they can typically speak a language with very little effort. These children don't even give the words that they use a second thought. They are native speakers.

However, it is very difficult for an adult to learn to speak a foreign language. Even after studying the language for 20 years, adults still never fully arrive at the same level of proficiency as a five year old native child.

The adult will still always speaks with an accent, and will still find themselves occasionally unsure of the proper verb conjugation, or unsure of what the word for something is.

128

The same thing occurs with values, morals, beliefs, ethics, and your child's overall worldview.

By the time that your child reaches their teenage years, the central beliefs and core values that form the foundation of how they believe that the world operates have all already been firmly set in their minds.

If you haven't taught them to be fluent with your own personal values, beliefs, morals, and ethics, then they likely will never reach the level of proficiency that you would have hoped.

Instead of having a native talent with these important values, they will always be just a little unsure. They may get very close to being perfect. But they will never quite be as comfortable with these skills as they would have been, had you started with them when they were very young children.

While my own children may still grumble when I inform them that they are going to spend an entire day working hard, they nevertheless get up and get to work.

They have learned through years of experience that it is futile to refuse to complete an assigned task. They have gained coping strategies for just bearing down and pushing through an unpleasant task.

If I had waited until they were 15 years old to start teaching them to work hard, do you think that I could have gotten them to work all day! The effort to do so would have utterly failed. They would have been useless lumps of human skin, dragging their feet through the day, and wasting my time, as I tried to work around them.

The same goes for sharing your worldview with your little ones. Whether that worldview is religion, politics, or the mores and traditions of your local community or culture.

In my case this worldview includes my membership in The Church of Jesus Christ of Latter-Day Saints.

From the time that my kids have been babies, we have attended weekly church services. We actively serve our local congregation through volunteering in a variety of positions, and most importantly we actively do our best to live our beliefs.

In our home, we try to read the scriptures together. We also try to pray together as a family. And once a week, we try to have a lesson, where mom or dad share some of our own personal thoughts and feelings about religion.

Notice that I said that we "try!" Because in all honesty, we don't always succeed. But we do the best that we can!

While driving in the car, or walking alone with a child, I often express my beliefs, feelings, and thoughts to them. I make sure that they are never left in doubt of exactly how I personally feel about a topic or issue.

How can you leave such a critical thing to chance! You are their dad!

Take the time to make sure that your kids know exactly how you feel regarding those things that are sacred and important to you. Then, when they are adults, they will be far more likely to care about the same things that you do.

At this point, it should be noted that your goal is never to force your children to believe the same things that you do. If you tried to force them, then you would almost certainly fail!

Rather, you are tenderly teaching, employing logic, and repeating again and again those lessons that are important to you.

If you have taught them in love, and above all set a proper example by practicing what you preach, then the odds are very high that one day your children's worldview will end up looking a lot like your own.

Even if your adult children do choose to reject some of the things that you taught them, and to live a lifestyle very different from that which you would have hoped that they would live. Then you will still find many opportunities to cheer for them.

For example, they may reject your religion, but perhaps they will still be hardworking and industrious.

They may choose not to participate in important cultural events that really matter to you, but even so, perhaps they will still treat their spouse and children with love and tenderness.

It was you who taught them those things! You didn't fail as a parent!

Rejoice in those lessons that they did learn!

It was you who taught them to work hard. It was you who taught them to love their life partner and their children.

It was you who taught them whatever other positive values that they exhibit.

Once they reach adulthood, you have to let go. Rejoice in who they are, love them for who they are, and work hard to build a strong lifelong relationship with them.

You don't have to condone their choices, but don't withhold your love, or your willingness to be apart of their life.

Celebrate those things that they did learn from you, and enjoy your relationship with them. Keep setting the example that you have always set, and remain true to those principles that matter to you.

As your children gain more life experience the odds are very high that in the end they will eventually return to the foundation that you built for them in childhood.

Even if they never do return. You will find great personal joy in those things that they did learn from you. More importantly, you will enjoy a lifelong friendship with them.

Teach your children to be successful in the adult world. Don't leave this important role to someone who does not share your own worldview.

Have patience. Understand that these lessons take many years to fully sink in. Repeat them again and again, be consistent, and set a proper example for them.

If they reject some of the things that you taught them, love them anyway! Continue to set a good example, and to build a strong relationship with them.

As you do these things, you will find great peace, joy, and a wonderful sense of happiness that will last throughout your entire life.

Chapter 10
Consistency Is What Counts In Fatherhood

Personal Story

The oppressive sun beat down on my face and neck. Causing me to grow more miserable with every step that I took.

Why were my parents making us trek so far out into the desert? I mean seriously! What was it about some old Indian ruins that was so important, that these ancient out of touch weirdos were hauling us hundreds of miles to see them?

135

And as if dragging me away from my friends wasn't bad enough, my Dad was droning on and on about.... well, I wasn't actually listening, but I am sure that whatever it was that he was talking about, it was boring!

I was more thirsty than I had ever been in my entire life, but unfortunately my old metal Boy Scout canteen had run out of water.

My feet hurt, and I really needed to rest! I glanced around, hoping to find a shady spot where I could sit down, or better yet hide out, but as I looked out across the desert all I could see was red hot dirt, and cacti stretching outward for miles.

I wasn't the only one who had noticed my near death condition. I was convinced that I could see vultures circling high above me, overhead. They were undoubtedly waiting for me to pass out, so that they could swoop down and begin pecking at my succulently roasted flesh.

This was it! This was where it was all going to end! I was going to die here in the New Mexico desert!

Yet as I listened incredulously to my father, who apparently didn't realize that we were all about to perish, he was still lecturing me!

I didn't know what was worse. The rock stuck in my shoe, or the old man's persistent monologue.

I could make a run for it! Maybe try to escape these old fossils who called themselves my parents! But where would I go?

Why did all my friends have normal parents, while I got stuck with these... desert wandering... nomads!

My friends were all probably at the air conditioned mall, or doing some other normal summer activity.

Their parents didn't haul them off to Mesa... where ever I was, and make them waste a perfectly good day getting slowly cooked into vulture pot roast.

If the vultures didn't eat me, then I was going to get stung by a scorpion, or bit by a rattlesnake! Didn't my parents even care about me!

My dad still blabbed on and on!

"and when your grandpa asked me why I was going to marry your mother, I told him that it was because I knew that she would be a good mother to you kids..."

Not that story again! He has told me that story already something like 300 times!! I wonder if he even remembers that he already told me that he married mom because she would be a good mother!

Sad how senile my dad is getting!

When I am a dad, I am NEVER going to drag my kids somewhere and lecture them while making them do something that they don't want to do!

I will never tell my kids the same story over and over and over!

Otter Lesson # 10
Otters Are Consistent

When it comes to rearing baby otters consistency is what makes all of the difference.

The adult otters begin teaching their otter pups from the moment that they are born and continue until they leave the den to strike it out on their own.

The same lessons are repeated again and again, because the pups need time for this knowledge to sink in. They also need time to practice the critical survival skills that they will someday use as adults to lead their own future bevies.

These skills include learning how to hunt, learning what is edible, how to build dens, how to use rocks to open shells, and how to behave in proper otter society.

Though there is much to learn about being an adult otter, I think that it is safe to say that there is far more to learn about being an adult human.

Important life lessons must be taught and retaught again and again, throughout childhood.

You can't say something once, and then expect that your children will remember it. Instead, you have to consistently repeat yourself, over a period of many years. Only then will they retain those lessons that you teach them.

Your children will undoubtedly become convinced that you are senile, boring, and repetitive. Just as I once thought that my own father was.

That is okay! Let them believe that you are old and boring. Years from now, once they have grown up a bit, your kids will incorporate those things that you most often repeated into their psyche.

Then, just as I now view my own father as the greatest example of manhood that I have ever known. So to will your children, one day understand why you taught them the way that you did.

Consistently repeating the same lessons, and consistently setting the same dependable example for your children has another important effect.

It will help you overcome those difficult moments, when you have no idea what you are doing as a parent!

As you do your best to guide your children through childhood, moments will inevitably arise when you will feel completely lost, confused, and unsure of what you are supposed to do as a parent.

You will ask yourself "what would my dad have done in this situation?"

Undoubtedly the situation that you will be facing with one of your children will be vastly different than anything that your parents ever had to deal with.

Unable to find parody between the challenge that you currently face, and those that beset your parents when they raised you, you will throw your arms up in resignation.

Lacking any example of what you are supposed to say or do, you will feel completely unsure of how you are supposed to proceed.

It is in these moments that you will wish that someone had given you a manual on how to raise kids when the doctor handed you your first baby in the hospital!

When you feel frustrated and unqualified to parent, remember this otter lesson.

It is the consistency that makes the difference to your children, not some magical thing that you say or do in any particular moment of trial.

Sometimes you will grasp at straws. Sometimes you will even make mistakes. You are not perfect! But guess what! Neither were your parents. They also made many mistakes in raising you.

Why don't you remember the mistakes that your parents made? Why do you hold your own parents up in your mind as the perfect models of what parents are supposed to be? Why did it always seem like they knew exactly what to do in every situation?

The answer to these questions is very straightforward.

Except in cases of neglect or abuse, we tend to forget our parent's mistakes. Years later when we think about them, we only remember that they were wise, and that they taught us how to be successful, well-balanced, productive adults.

While we forget, or far more often didn't even notice those moments when they were grasping at straws, we clearly remember the lessons that they repeated ten thousand times throughout our childhoods.

The fact that our parents got up every day and worked hard. The stories that they repeated so many times to anyone who would listen to them. The faithful and consistent examples that they always set for us.

True there are some more poignant moments from each of our childhoods that stand out in our memories. An occasion when a bit of well timed advice made all of the difference for us.

Undoubtedly that advice has repeatedly circled around inside our minds throughout our adult lives, causing us to marvel at the wisdom that our parents displayed. We may even ask ourselves, how did our parents know that this advice was exactly what we needed to hear in that particular moment.

But those magical inspirational moments are not something that you can plan, nor are your parents likely even aware that they occurred.

Almost without exception they probably gave the same advice ten, fifty, or a hundred times before. The moment that you recall with fondness just happens to be the time that this often repeated advice finally actually sunk in.

Which is why that particular moment lives in your long term memory, while all the other times that they said the exact same thing have all been forgotten.

Don't ever doubt that you have what it takes to raise your own children.

The Lord sent you these precious little spirits. He knows you, and he knows them. He knows your personality, and he knows their personalities. You are the father that these particular children will best relate and respond to. Your personality is exactly what these little ones need.

As long as you are neither neglectful nor abusive, and if you truly do your best, then you will get through those mystical moments when there is no clear path forward.

The question of whether your actions, lectures, or punishments were too soft, or too hard will become distant and irrelevant memories.

Your children won't remember your mistakes. They will instead internalize those lessons that you consistently taught them

After 20 years in your home, they will be ready to face the world, and to do so in a manner that will bring you great joy and pride.

Be consistent!
Then trust that the more difficult moments will work themselves out!

Conclusion

Otters may just be lowly rodents, unaware of such humanly pursuits as philosophy, technology, or science. However, their simple lives, which they dedicate to family, and predicate upon affection and love, greatly elevate their stature among God's creations.

They may never read Shakespeare, nor comprehend the nuclear reactions taking place overhead in the Sun. However they have something that may very well be far more significant and profound. Otters are happy!

The same universal principles that lead a sea otter towards happiness will operate on you or any other individual.

Ten Otter Lessons That Lead To A Life of Obnoxious Happiness

1. It's Dangerous To Swim Alone

2. Otters Are Fiercely Monogamous

3. Otters Don't Criticize Each Other

4. Only A Stupid Otter Refuses Extra Oysters!

5. Otters Are Remarkably Good At Keeping Confidences

6. An Otter's Primary Purpose Is To Bring Forth And Prepare The Next Generation of Otters

7. Otters Don't Have Any Money! Yet Somehow They Thrive.

8. When They Are Not Busy, Otters Can Almost Always Be Found Snuggling!

9. Adult Otters Teach Young Otters How To Survive In The Wild

10. Otters are consistent

As I conclude this work, I want to add one final caution, which is critical to understand if you are truly going to live an obnoxiously happy life.

Give yourself permission to mess up, make mistakes, and start over again!

You are not perfect. You are going to mess up! At some point, no matter how hard you try, you are going to let yourself down.

Or perhaps you are finding this book late in life, and have already built up years of missed opportunities and regrets.

It is unquestionably better to start young. Doing so will absolutely have a profound impact on your life. However, this does not mean that if you are old, that it is too late to begin today to live a happier lifestyle.

Happiness Is A Continuum.

The level to which you live the principles governing happiness will determine where on that continuum you stand.

Mistakes will set you back a bit and make you feel slightly less happy. But slightly less happy is still very happy!

Yes, starting late means that you are starting at the bottom of the happiness continuum, and have far less time to climb to the top. But with every step that you take your life will improve, and you will feel more joy.

Regardless of where you find yourself today, just keep moving forward.

About The Author

Hiram J. Bertoch

Hiram lives in Hunter, Utah with his wife Anna and their seven children.

Hiram has authored five books, including the regional best seller The Mountain Christians.

Hiram founded The KidsKnowIt Network, which today is the most successful international educational resource in the world serving hundreds of millions of children worldwide.

Throughout his career Hiram has served on various boards, and in leadership positions for a variety of companies and organizations. He volunteers as both the President of The Board of Trustees, and also as the Sexton for the Pleasant Green Cemetery, an historic pioneer cemetery in the Oquirrh Mountains, overlooking the Salt Lake Valley.

Hiram teaches middle school science in a local Salt Lake Area school, and loves every second of it! As well as all of his students!!

18816003R00090

Printed in Great Britain
by Amazon